Extreme Faith Workout

How to Stop Being a Couch Potato Christian

Branddon A. Mays

sermontobook
.com

Sermon To Book
www.sermontobook.com

Extreme Faith Workout / Branddon A. Mays
ISBN-13: 9780692747582
ISBN-10: 0692747583

I would like to dedicate this book to my family, especially my wonderful mother, the late Yvonne Mays, my father William A. Fairley, my aunt Evelyn Abron, and the late Rev. Raymond Mays, Sr., who was my very first pastor.

To my leader Bishop Norman E. Hardman, Sr., a strong man of faith who has taught me how to become the champion God created me to be, and that giving up is not an option. You have helped me to discover and walk in my God-given purpose, and how to teach the Word with accuracy.

To Dr. Jerry A. Grillo, Jr., for writing the foreword for my book.

To the late Apostle Horace Leonard, who helped groom me for ministry.

To the late Evangelist Earnestine Hunt.

To my Revamp Church Family, whom I love with all my heart. You have been a great support system.

To the covenant partners and friends who have supported me through my years of ministry. I pray the blessings of the Lord over your lives for your continued support.

CONTENTS

Dr. Jerry A. Grillo, Jr.

Foreword

Every situation in life is attempting to sabotage your focus, your faith, and your desires. When you lose your focus, you lose your direction. When you lose your faith, you lose the ability to move beyond the power of hope, peace, and recovery. When you lose your desire, you lose the passion to stay on course.

In Dr. Branddon Mays's newest book, "Extreme Faith Workout," you are going to be propelled into your future. Faith is a spiritual muscle that has to be trained, stretched, and pushed against. Your life becomes a permanent struggle if you don't learn how to build your faith, increase your faith, and move your faith. Dr. Mays gives you the information you require to train your mind, rewire your habits, and build your success principles. You will learn how to focus your faith, calm your anxieties, motivate your purpose, and equip your mind to move forward into your dreams and visions.

This is the book you've been waiting for. I recommend that you read this book slowly and methodically. Absorb its truths. There will be at least one key in this manuscript that's going to revolutionize your life—document them for change.

Dr. Jerry A. Grillo, Jr.
Author, Speaker, Pastor

WELCOME

Note from the Author

Thank you for purchasing *Extreme Faith Workout*!

Accompanying each main chapter of the book is a set of reflective questions with a practical, application-oriented action step. These workbook sections are a tool to help you get off the spiritual couch and start exercising your faith as never before.

I recommend you go through these workbook sections with a pen in order to write your thoughts and record notes in the areas provided. The questions are suitable for independent reflection, discussion with a friend, or review with a study group.

Regardless of what led you to this book or how you choose to approach it, I hope that the experience of reading and reflecting on it helps you practice an active, faith-filled life.

INTRODUCTION

Get Off the Couch!

Faith is like a muscle.

We all have the same muscles, but our bodies look very different from each other. One of the reasons for that is because some of us work out and develop our muscles, while others are rather less active! Yet even the most dedicated couch potato can begin to build their fitness level, increase their muscle tone, and change their appearance beyond all recognition.

In the same way, we start out on our Christian journey with just a little bit of faith. Maybe we're not quite sure how much we can believe and trust our Heavenly Father, so we have to learn by experience that He will never let us down. This may take us some time. In fact, many of us spend a whole lifetime learning just that one simple truth.

This book is about experiencing life as an extreme faith workout—about exercising our faith muscles on a daily basis, because the more we use them the stronger and more powerful they become. Just like the couch potato, faith can transform us so that we hardly recognize ourselves! It all starts with understanding what Jesus has done for us, learning how to follow Him, and putting our faith into action.

Of course, our beliefs are important, but sometimes it's about more than just believing. Our dedicated couch potato can believe in exercise, but it is only once he gets off of that sofa and starts to move about that his belief makes any difference to his waistline!

In the same way, faith needs to be put into practice in order to grow and develop; it needs to be more than just an abstract idea if you are to be used effectively by our Heavenly Father. The Bible tells us that "...without faith it is impossible to please Him..." (Hebrews 11:6) and "Faith comes by hearing, and hearing by the word of God" (Romans 10:17). That's not to say, however, that if your faith is weak He isn't interested in you; even faith as tiny as a mustard seed can be powerful enough to move mountains (Matthew 17:20). So although our faith may be weak at times, God is able to use it to great effect if we remain rooted in Him.

Putting our faith into action is an amazing journey, one with its own ups and downs. There will be blessings and joys, but also times of trouble when our faith is tested. However, when we walk with the Lord every day we can not only survive, but *grow* in faith through the times of struggle and adversity we face.

So if you are ready to start out on this extreme faith workout journey, or are looking for a little support along the way, this book will help you understand what happens once we commit ourselves to Him in faith and start to use our new muscles—because faith is just the start, and it leads to so much more.

CHAPTER ONE

Taking Your First Steps

Imagine a growing baby who has got to the stage where he starts learning to walk unaided. Pulling himself up on the furniture, he eventually manages to totter a short way before sitting down with a bump. Fortunately, he usually has a soft landing thanks to his diaper and is soon ready to try again. Failure doesn't mean he gives up! He's too young to understand balance or gravity, or even to have a fear of falling, but instinct will mean he keeps trying until he is able to walk like mommy and daddy.

Now picture a different learning-to-walk scenario. This time it's an adult who has been seriously injured in a car crash. In due course, once the injuries have healed, the patient will need physical therapy to build up his muscles. Then he will need to learn to walk again. Like the baby, he may only manage tiny steps, but this time he knows all too well about falling. He might fear the pain;

he certainly fears the failure. It will take a great deal of determination to learn to walk a second time.

For the baby, learning to walk is an amazing achievement given his size and age. For the adult, it's also an amazing achievement given everything he has to put himself through, and no doubt there are many who give up the struggle and resign themselves to life in a wheelchair.

Neither the baby nor the adult can manage on his own; they have a whole support system around them, both physically and emotionally. However, the desire to walk comes from within; without that urge to stand up and walk, they would never see the world from a different level. That is the same as Christians who decide they want to grow in their faith and develop their relationship with our Heavenly Father.

We might identify more with the toddler if we have yet to step out in faith, or we may feel we are more like the accident victim if we crashed and burned last time. Either way, it's time to pull ourselves to our feet and try again. Like daddy with the baby, God will be holding our hand all the way; like the therapist with the car crash victim, He will be right there, strengthening our muscles and encouraging us to take one more step—while providing backup in case we fall.

In the Psalms, we read:

The LORD makes firm the steps of the one who delights in him; though he may stumble, he will not

fall, for the LORD upholds him with His hand —
Psalm 37:23-24 (NIV)

As we begin to step out in faith, He will be upholding us every day.

Practicing What We Preach

What does it mean to live by faith? How do we exercise faith so that it will grow and become stronger?

As Christians, we believe that God offers us forgiveness for all we have done wrong through the death of his Son, Jesus Christ. God has promised that when we repent, He will accept Christ's death in our place so we can live in fellowship with Him forever. Jesus has wiped the slate clean so we can be truly born again. Isn't that amazing?

Deciding to believe and accept is the first step to having faith in God's promises. Faith often begins as a decision, although some people experience an overwhelming certainty as they commit themselves to God's care. Either way, it's just the beginning of the journey!

The more we get to know our Heavenly Father, the more we learn to trust Him and believe His Word. We learn that we can act on His promises and obey His prompting because we can have complete confidence in Him in every situation. When we reflect on the lessons of the past, we come to understand that the future is

securely held in His hands. Just look at the beauty of
creation, read the promises in Scripture, and talk to other
Christians about their experience of His faithfulness if
you are in any doubt at all.

Faith reassures us of God's loving kindness and
guides us through the whole of our Christian life. It gives
us hope, makes us bold, and strengthens us to keep going
when times are hard.

Faith is about putting our beliefs into practice—
provided, of course, that our beliefs are rooted in His
Word. Some people hold very strong beliefs, but that
doesn't mean they necessarily have a Bible-based faith.

Just because we believe in something doesn't mean it
must be true. We could leap off a building and believe
we could fly, but it would end in disaster! This kind of
misguided belief is not what faith is about. Instead, it
must be centered on God's Word and be rooted in His
love.

Not-So-Blind Faith

Is faith blind? Or is there something more to it?

Faith is more than an emotion, and Christianity is
more than a set of personal beliefs. It is not a fairytale; it
is based on real historical evidence. And although
Christianity is a major world religion, the kind of faith
we are talking about here is more than just going to
church on Sunday. It is not about habits or even about

feelings; it is instead about a relationship, knowing who God is as revealed through His Word.

The Bible we have today is not one book, but a library of sixty-six books written over many centuries. The many different authors were inspired by the Holy Spirit, often at great risk to themselves, and had no idea of the significant part they would play in teaching future generations about God. On top of that, just consider the millions of personal testimonies and thousands of volumes of works by more recent authors and teachers. We have an amazing body of knowledge to draw upon.

The Bible teaches us about God, about faith, and about ourselves. It shows us that although we need to have the simple, trusting faith of a child, faith itself is not as straightforward. James tells us that "even the demons believe—and tremble" (James 2:19). And although it is about trust, faith is not blind trust in a vague, beneficent being, nor is it a kind of spiritual version of crossing your fingers and hoping for the best. It is about a close personal relationship with our loving Heavenly Father through the blood of Jesus Christ.

When we don't see the way ahead, faith means trusting and believing anyway. In fact, the whole concept of our Christian faith is a blend of belief and trust. It is not just believing *about*, but believing *in*. So before we go any further, let me ask you: Is your faith like that? Or do your faith muscles need a little exercise before you get to that point?

A Two-Way Street

Dr. Richard J. Krejcir says, "Faith is a two-way street; we receive it from God, and respond it back as trust. It would be like a lake which has a source and an outlet. If we only have an outlet we would dry up. If we just have a source we become like the Dead Sea, lifeless and void."[1]

Faith demands a response; it is not just a comfortable emotion or an abstract belief system. Because we have confidence in God and in His plan and purpose for our lives, we can put our faith into action instead of leaving it in a drawer and only taking it out on Sundays.

When we are truly walking with Him, He will show us how to put our faith into action every day. It could mean taking small steps, like sharing with someone who is struggling under their burden, maybe learning how to support them—practically as well as spiritually. Or it could mean taking big leaps, like giving up a well-paid job to work with those who have nothing—even moving to work in a developing country. Or it may mean just carrying on in difficult circumstances; sometimes this is the hardest task of all.

Whatever your situation now, or whatever you may be called to do in the future, you can have complete confidence in God's faithfulness. He will never let you down.

In 1 John 5:5 we read, "Who is he who overcomes the world, but he who believes that Jesus is the Son of God?"

(1 John 5:5). Even if you have only just started to trust in Him, your weak faith in our almighty God is the strongest force on earth!

WORKBOOK

Chapter 1 Questions

Question: At what stage of faith are you today? What is your faith grounded in?

_____
_____
_____
_____
_____
_____
_____
_____
_____
_____
_____
_____

Question: In what areas of life do you struggle to trust God? How specifically will you improve your trust?

_____

_____

_____

_____

_____

_____

_____

_____

_____

_____

_____

_____

_____

Action: Today, take your first steps in a more active faith! Respond to your faith in (and from) God by trusting confidently in Him. Let God show you how to live each day in faith.

Chapter 1 Notes

_____

_____

_____

_____

_____

_____

_____

_____

_____

_____

_____

_____

_____

_____

_____

_____

_____

_____

_____

_____

_____

_____

_____

_____

CHAPTER TWO

The Amazing Power of Grace

I recently heard about a man in a far-off city who joined a group of fellow Christians for Bible study. To his dismay, he heard them discussing the Crucifixion as though it were no big deal. These people all agreed that Jesus knew He would rise again on the third day because He had predicted it to His disciples several times. Death on the cross was merely an unpleasant, short-term ordeal.

The man was horrified and tried to explain that, by taking the wrath of His Father on Himself, Jesus was accepting more than a horrible death; He also suffered the spiritual agony of separation from God and punishment for every sin the world has ever known. Sadly, the other members of the group were unconvinced and the man never went back.

My friend, never underestimate the price Christ paid for your sins. It wasn't easy. We sometimes take it for granted, especially if we have spent many years going to church, but redemption came at a great price. Our selfish desire to go our own way, even now, is an insult to Him like a slap in the face, and something we need to deal with if we want our Heavenly Father to be able to work through us.

Too Good Not to Be True

In order to understand fully what faith in God through Jesus Christ means to us, in this chapter we are going to look at a crucial time in the history of the Church in the last five hundred years: the Reformation. What was it and why was it so important?

The Reformation was a major turning point in Church history. The established Catholic Church had governed every area of people's lives for centuries, but the voices of dissent gradually became a torrent that washed its power aside, eventually bringing the freedom of religion to many countries. Those who had protested gave their name to what became the Protestant Church (now the umbrella term for most non-Catholic churches), and the key area was the issue of salvation.

Theologians have debated the role we play in our salvation for centuries. Because the Bible tells us so, we know that we are saved by God's grace through the death and resurrection of Christ. But the accepted thinking by the Catholic Church was that something more was needed. Maybe it sounded too simplistic, or even too good to be true. Maybe they noticed a tendency among believers to accept the message of God's salvation and then carry on behaving as they wanted. Or possibly the

Church leaders saw their own roles as powerful intermediaries in danger of being eclipsed by the message of God's grace, freely given to all.

Therefore, according to the Catholic Church, we are in the process of being saved through a combination of our faith and the sacraments, as received through the Church. Faith alone is not enough, they say.

The Reformers were no longer prepared to accept this teaching. Instead, they stressed that, according to Scripture, we are saved as soon as we believe in God's gift of grace, the death of His Son on the cross. This is a cornerstone of first-century Christian teaching that is repeated in many Biblical passages.

While Paul and Silas are imprisoned at Philippi, they spend their time singing and praying to God. During the night there is an earthquake that makes the prison doors spring open. The jailor assumes every prisoner will have escaped and prepares to kill himself in shame, but Paul calls out to him that everyone is still there. "Sirs, what must I do to be saved?" he asks. "Believe on the Lord Jesus Christ, and you will be saved, you and your household" (Acts 16:31), Paul tells him.

So the focus of the Reformation was the emphasis on justification by faith—that is, we are made right with God entirely because we believe that Jesus's death and resurrection have saved us from our sins, according to His promise. Prominent figures like Luther and Calvin, among many others, had read the Word of God and came to believe this so strongly that they dared to challenge the establishment: the Catholic Church. Over the following centuries, many brave Christians were tortured and killed in horrible ways for believing in justification by faith—also known as salvation by grace. Grace is that important!

One Grace Covers All

God's grace is a "get out of jail" card, a free pardon that says our punishment for sin has been paid by someone else—in much the same way as a stranger may sometimes pay for someone's meal or toll charge as a random act of kindness, but on a cosmic scale! The things we do that are selfish or cruel or uncaring—our sins that mean we fall short of His perfect standards—would have separated us from God forever, because we would eventually have to pay the penalty, but God's grace has wiped them away.

There is *nothing* we could ever do to earn this pardon. The Bible tells us, "For by grace you have been saved through faith, and that not of yourselves; it is the gift of God, not of works, lest anyone should boast" (Ephesians 2:8-9).

What is even more amazing about grace is that there is nothing we need to add to it! We don't have to earn our salvation: It is a gift from God our Father. If we fall into sin again, even if we do it deliberately, He will forgive us every time we truly repent. That's because He has accepted the sacrifice Jesus made on the cross once and for all time.

Like a blanket, Jesus's blood covers us from the anger and punishment of a righteous God. This is called *atonement*—Jesus atoned for our sins by taking the wrath of the Father upon Himself. As Psalm 103:12 tells us, "As far as the east is from the west, so far has He removed our transgressions from us."

No wonder Jesus spoke to Nicodemus about the need to be born again: "Most assuredly, I say to you, unless one is born of water and the Spirit, he cannot enter the kingdom of God" (John 3:5). If you are setting out on your journey into faith, bear in mind that your human nature will fight you every step of the way. Spiritual growth first calls for a spiritual rebirth.

Sharing the Love

Of course the truth is that, although we are saved by grace and not by anything we do, we would expect to see a life change in anyone who accepts this wonderful gift and commits their life to the Lord. This is because our faith should be producing fruit, changes in our attitudes and even our personality, which bless the church and the wider community.

Paul lists this fruit in Galatians 5. "But the fruit of the Spirit is love, joy, peace, longsuffering, kindness, goodness, faithfulness, gentleness, self-control" (Galatians 5:22-23). The first one on the list is love for others—not a cozy emotion, but a powerful force for good that translates in numerous practical ways. James writes, "For as the body without the spirit is dead, so faith without works is dead also" (James 2:26).

These works, or practical deeds, are not a condition of salvation as the Catholic Church teaches, but an expression of our love for God and for other people. They are faith in action. If your life, behavior, and attitudes have not changed as a result of accepting Jesus's sacrifice on your behalf, it does not mean that you have not been justified and accepted by God—but you need to ask yourself why you haven't changed at all. Maybe He has something more for you.

In the New Testament, the outward expression of faith through acts of kindness and compassion is the norm, from the story Jesus told in the parable of the Good Samaritan to the hospitality shown to Paul and his companions by the early Christian converts.

Ultimately, faith alone is what saves us, but faith needs to be exercised through works—otherwise, it's missing something.

WORKBOOK

Chapter 2 Questions

Question: Do you think about doing good as a way to earn or deserve salvation, or as an expression of your faith?

_____

_____

_____

_____

_____

_____

_____

_____

_____

_____

_____

_____

Question: How does your faith show through your daily words and actions?

_____

_____

_____

_____

_____

_____

_____

_____

_____

_____

_____

_____

Action: Take confidence that God's grace covers all of your sins. But don't stop there! Let your faith and His grace shine through you to transform your daily life. Love others with more than cozy emotions. Rather, actively care for them by practicing and demonstrating all the fruits of the Spirit.

Chapter 2 Notes

_____

_____

_____

_____

_____

_____

_____

_____

_____

_____

_____

_____

_____

_____

_____

_____

_____

_____

_____

_____

_____

_____

_____

CHAPTER THREE

When the Going Gets Tough

We all hope for a wide variety of things, don't we? Sometimes it may be just an idle thought; we might say, "I hope it's pizza for dinner," or "I hope it doesn't rain tomorrow." But at other times hope is a powerful emotion, sometimes even too big to put into words, that affects and colors everything we do. An example of this kind of hope could be while waiting for life or death medical results from a hospital or clinic, or when a childless woman desperately longs for a baby. It's sometimes called "hoping against hope."

The Bible tells us that faith produces hope. Hebrews 11:1 tells us that "faith is the substance of things hoped for" (Hebrews 11:1). What does that mean? It seems to be a contradiction—how can something be physically present and yet not be there, just hoped for in the future? In fact, this verse tells us a lot about both faith and hope.

In Scripture, hope is not an idle thought or even a devout wish. Instead, it is about a certainty, the eternal love between God and His children, and usually refers to God's faithfulness. The Psalmist says in Psalm 71, "For You are my hope, O Lord GOD; You are my trust from my youth" (Psalm 71:5). He has learned from experience that trusting in God is never a mistake.

When we believe in His forgiveness and redemption through Jesus's death on the cross, we begin to have hope in our lives. This hope leads to joy and strengthens our faith even more. Hope in the Bible is about the future, when we will be with Jesus Christ in glory according to His promises, but it's also about today—a source of strength for our everyday lives on earth.

Imagine a young man who has a wealthy elderly relative, and he knows he is set to inherit a lot of money from this relative in due course. Knowing he will be rich one day certainly makes a big difference to his life and his plans for the future. But suppose Granny changed her will, or even worse, gave the money to someone else without telling him? What a cruel joke that would be! So until he actually inherits it, the young man can never know for sure, and his hope for the future will always be tinged with anxiety.

Now imagine that this large sum of money is already left for him in a trust fund. The money is his; no one else can take it away. He only has to wait until he reaches the age chosen by his relative. His future is secure, and although he may have some difficulties until then, he can live without fear or anxiety for the years ahead. *That* is what the Bible means by hope: Not a vague wish, an anxious possibility, or a desperate longing, but a firm expectation.

Eyes on the Prize

I press on toward the goal to win the prize for which God has called me heavenward in Christ Jesus. — **Philippians 3:14 (NIV)**

Have you noticed that the more you look at your problems, the worse they seem? That is because when our focus is on ourselves and our situation, we often feel things are pretty dire.

It is all too easy to take our eyes off Jesus and instead see things as the world sees them. Just as Peter stepped out of the boat to walk toward Him on the water, once we focus on the storm around us, we start to sink. We can only hold onto this attitude of hope, a firm expectation based on the promises of God, by remaining close to Jesus and having our eyes focused upon Him.

Paul tells us that when things get tough, it's an opportunity to experience God's love as we continue to trust in Him. In Romans 5, we read:

Therefore, having been justified by faith, we have peace with God through our Lord Jesus Christ, through whom also we have access by faith into this

grace in which we stand, and rejoice in hope of the glory of God. And not only that, but we also glory in tribulations, knowing that tribulation produces perseverance; and perseverance, character; and character, hope. Now hope does not disappoint, because the love of God has been poured out in our hearts by the Holy Spirit who was given to us. —
Romans 5:1-5

Hope gives us the strength to be patient and confident as we seek to serve God and His Church in whatever way He shows us. When things get difficult, hope keeps our eyes fixed on Him. It even grows through the hard times and helps us to keep going. And, as Paul says, hope does not leave us disappointed, because it is the means for God's love to be poured out in our hearts.

Persevering in Jesus's Footsteps

In Romans 8:25, Paul adds: "If we hope for what we do not see, we eagerly wait for it with perseverance" (Romans 8:25). Picture two children growing up in separate families; one child is overindulged, the other has very little. In the first family, a loving father gives his child everything he or she could ever want. What happens? That child does not learn to "wait with perseverance." Instead, they expect everything to fall into their lap without delay!

Conversely, the second child has never received anything. What does he expect? Nothing! Someone who has never been given anything has no hope for the future and has trouble believing any promises.

But God is not like either of those fathers. He doesn't indulge our every whim, but neither does He deprive us of good things. Because of who He is and what He has promised, we know some of what He will reveal in the future for us, but for the moment we have to wait. That is how faith produces hope.

In Hebrews we read of how hope leads us ever closer to God. "This hope we have as an anchor of the soul, both sure and steadfast, and which enters the Presence behind the veil." The writer goes on to explain how this strong, certain hope leads us in Jesus's footsteps, right into God's presence: "Where the forerunner has entered for us, even Jesus, having become High Priest forever according to the order of Melchizedek" (Hebrews 6:19-20).

Just like the fortunate young man with the trust fund, we have a great inheritance in store for us. Many years after he stepped out of the boat to walk on the water toward the Savior, Peter was facing danger of another kind: imprisonment and death for his ongoing ministry to the first-century churches. He wrote these faith-filled words:

> *Blessed be the God and Father of our Lord Jesus Christ, who according to His abundant mercy has begotten us again to a living hope through the resurrection of Jesus Christ from the dead, to an*

inheritance incorruptible and undefiled and that does not fade away, reserved in heaven for you. — 1 Peter 1:3-4

If at times you face despair and maybe experience a devastating sense of hopelessness, don't panic, and above all, don't lose your trust in our Heavenly Father! Remember, on our faith journey we are not guided by our feelings, but by the knowledge and love of God, and He is always there.

As Dr. Richard J. Krejcir puts it:

> If you feel you have no hope, then you have no vision, no purpose, no trust, and no faith in the One who loves you. Hope allows you to live with the perspective of eternity, so you are not bogged down in your dire circumstances.[2]

This "sure and steadfast hope" is truly an anchor in a topsy-turvy world. When circumstances threaten to overwhelm us, His loving kindness is unchanging.

WORKBOOK

Chapter 3 Questions

Question: When has God been faithful to lift you out of hopelessness or despair?

_____
_____
_____
_____
_____
_____
_____
_____
_____
_____
_____
_____

Question: How can you keep your eyes on Jesus during difficult times?

_____

_____

_____

_____

_____

_____

_____

_____

_____

_____

_____

_____

Action: Practice a sure and steadfast hope! Be confident in your salvation as you fix your eyes on Jesus and His promises. Let your certain hope lead you closer to God as you persevere in Jesus's footsteps.

Chapter 3 Notes

_____

_____

_____

_____

_____

_____

_____

_____

_____

_____

_____

_____

_____

_____

_____

_____

_____

_____

_____

_____

_____

_____

_____

_____

CHAPTER FOUR

Total Faithfulness

Great is Thy faithfulness, O God my Father...Thou changest not, Thy compassions they fail not, as Thou hast been, Thou forever wilt be!...Morning by morning new mercies I see...[3]

God never lets us down—ever. He is faithful to save those of us who believe in Him, even though we don't deserve His gift of salvation. And because of God's faithfulness toward us, we experience a sure and steady hope for the future.

So how do we respond to all of these incredible gifts? What about our faithfulness toward Him?

As we saw in the last chapter, Paul lists the fruit of the Spirit in his letter to the Galatians:

But the fruit of the Spirit is love, joy, peace, longsuffering, kindness, goodness, faithfulness,

gentleness, self-control. Against such there is no law.
— *Galatians 5:22-23*

If someone is faithful, they could be described as *loyal and committed.* It's about being in it for the long haul, standing firm under temptation or pressure, and being reliable. We expect to find (and demonstrate) this faithfulness with our marriage partner, with our friends, and hopefully, with our business associates. In fact, we might even take it for granted, just as we can often take God's faithfulness for granted, and forget to thank Him for never letting us down.

What about the other way round? Can He take you for granted? I believe that most of us, if we are being honest, would have to answer "no." We are fallible and make mistakes; even the best of us are very far from perfect. Fortunately, our Heavenly Father knows us very well, and is ready and willing to help us stand firm and be faithful.

When we look again at Paul's list of the fruit of the Spirit, we see that the majority are designed to bless our brothers and sisters in the church and the wider community. Only *joy* and *peace* might seem to be directed inward to bless ourselves more than outwards, a reflection of our relationship with the Father. And faithfulness? It could be described as our response to Him, directed upward; it is something we give back to God.

Faithful in Tribulation

As we saw in Chapter 3, there are times when we can become overwhelmed, discouraged, or scared by the situation we find ourselves in. At such times our faith can wobble and we may tell ourselves God doesn't care. We might even doubt His existence.

The reason for that is when we take our eyes off Jesus, we see how big the storm is all around us, like Peter walking on the water toward Him. Whatever your scary situation, it's hardly surprising that losing focus at such times means our trust in God may fail, or we might wonder if He really is in control.

I believe our Heavenly Father knows that we are weaklings. A temporary faith-wobble is understandable, but losing confidence in Him can mean we miss out on the amazing solution He has in mind to resolve even the most difficult of circumstances. So if your faith is faltering, cry out to Him—and be honest about it!

Bryan, a man in late middle age, proclaimed himself to be an atheist because as a child he'd prayed for his sick granny, yet she died. A tragic story, not least because the little boy could still be glimpsed, bewildered and confused, in the cranky older man. When God didn't answer his prayers, the boy told himself that obviously He didn't exist—whereas, of course, he continued to blame God for the rest of his life, so he was not really an atheist at all.

Are we like that? I think there are times when we all expect God to answer our prayers, no matter how immature or unreasonable, in just the way we want. When we don't get our own way, it can hurt and confuse us, but we need to learn from the experience. Above all, we must not let it damage our relationship with our Heavenly Father. He is always faithful toward us—just think of all the references in the Psalms alone to His mercy and His loving kindness—yet all too often we don't choose to be faithful toward Him.

Often we give up waiting for God's timing, and there are many times when we fail to be faithful because of our own selfishness or laziness. That is usually because we have a worldly idea of time; we want things to happen right away, instead of learning to persevere in prayer and be steadfast in hope. When things don't happen the way we want, we need to take the opportunity to learn from the situation. Remaining faithful means making a bit of an effort!

By contrast, Arnold was a faithful brother who lived a long life in service to God. In his eighties, when many people would be thinking about taking it easy, he was involved in planting a new church in a small country village. Every week, he was among half a dozen Christians who sat round a table praying for this tiny church plant. When they began to get discouraged, he would exhort them to "just hold on." Thanks largely to his faithfulness and encouragement, they continued to persevere in prayer and waiting upon the Lord, and the little church has grown from five or six people to eighty-eight—a sizeable congregation in such a rural location.

Quietly Committed to Serve

Although faithfulness is something we offer to God, it can also be such a blessing to other people. Contrary to popular thinking and the ways of this world, we need to put others first and stop thinking of ourselves. It's true that sometimes we might need to put ourselves forward in faith, but many times faithfulness takes place in the shadows, away from the limelight.

James and John, two of Jesus's disciples, didn't get this. To the indignation of the others, they asked Jesus for a special favor. "Grant us that we may sit, one on Your right hand and the other on Your left, in Your glory," they asked (Mark 10:37). I guess they can be commended for their utter belief in His kingdom, although they got everything else wrong! Jesus gently sets them right:

> *Whoever desires to become great among you shall be your servant. And whoever of you desires to be first shall be slave of all. For even the Son of Man did not come to be served, but to serve, and to give His life a ransom for many.* — ***Mark 10:43-45***

There are people helping in your church every week who are faithful in quiet acts of service. They may do the cleaning, or tidy up after services and other activities. They may provide refreshments or bake cakes or sweep the path. Do you know who they are? There are people who lovingly support others in prayer for years, who spend time with the lonely or bring elderly people to church every week, and often no one even notices. Faithfulness is such a powerful characteristic, yet it is often invisible to everyone but God.

You can be quite sure that anything that puts "me" at the center will be contrary to the Word of God, and will never bring blessing and healing to those around us. Instead, we have to remember that the Lord must be at the center of everything, and if He wants us to be edged aside to give way to someone or something else, so be it. It's another opportunity to learn about faithfulness!

Once we begin to seek faithfulness, our Heavenly Father is able to work within us and use us more to benefit others. We will learn more about Him and about ourselves, and we'll be able to respond to His prompting. He has much bigger things in mind for those who prove faithful, and we need to remember it next time we bring our list of requests and complaints before Him!

That does not mean we should not take our concerns and worries to God. Of course we can! David said, "I pour out my complaint before Him…I said, 'You are my refuge, my portion in the land of the living. Attend to my cry, for I am brought very low'" (Psalm 142:2, 5-6).

But sometimes we can end up using prayer as a kind of shopping list, or as an excuse to complain about our brothers and sisters, among others. And in that case, the only answer we receive may well be a gentle reminder about being so concerned over a "speck" in our brother's eye that we fail to notice the "plank" in our own eye (Matthew 7:3).

Faithfulness is a great opportunity to grow closer to our loving Heavenly Father as we seek to serve Him and others without expecting anything in return—except more evidence of His loving kindness!

WORKBOOK

Chapter 4 Questions

Question: When has God's timing proven to be better than your timing? How can you reinforce your commitment to waiting on God's timing in the future?

_____

_____

_____

_____

_____

_____

_____

_____

_____

_____

_____

Question: How can you quietly serve God and others, without drawing attention to yourself?

_____

_____

_____

_____

_____

_____

_____

_____

_____

_____

_____

_____

Action: Remain faithful during challenging and difficult times as you wait on God's timing for deliverance. Meanwhile, commit yourself to serving God and others patiently and quietly, outside of the limelight.

Chapter 4 Notes

_____

_____

_____

_____

_____

_____

_____

_____

_____

_____

_____

_____

_____

_____

_____

_____

_____

_____

_____

_____

_____

_____

_____

CHAPTER FIVE

The Power of Optimism

As we exercise our faith, our relationship with God gives rise to hope and faithfulness. No matter the situation we find ourselves in, or the dangers and difficulties we face, we know that He is there with us and that "all things work together for good to those…who are the called according to His purpose" (Romans 8:28).

This knowledge must surely give us a positive, optimistic outlook on life! What could be more wonderful than to know everything will be all right in the end?

Well, it may surprise you to learn that some Christians are less than optimistic about life. In fact, quite a lot of us just plod on with our daily activities and don't feel particularly excited about what God may be doing around us. Sometimes we don't seem to have the energy to be enthusiastic when it comes to supporting the next church program or evangelical outreach.

If that sounds like you, I would suggest that you could be losing your focus. It is all too easy to become so busy with work, family, church, and other valid, laudable activities that we don't have time to raise our eyes and look at the bigger picture, the one that God sees—his vision for our neighborhood, for our city. Of course He is intimately concerned with every individual within our community, but His plans are never limited to one person at a time.

We can all too easily become distracted; we get sidetracked doing things that are important, but not the most important. Sometimes even the best Christian leaders are swamped under a tide of administration and minor practical issues. Alternatively, if you are one of the faithful who is always ready to volunteer at every church activity but feel your energy is flagging, could you be in danger of burnout? Either way, we need to learn to focus on what really matters.

Negativity in the Church

Spiritual optimism is when hope and faithfulness combine to produce an energetic confidence that God is in control and He will ensure that everything works out for the best—even when that turns out to be not quite what we had in mind! He sees the bigger picture, after all.

Optimism lets us see the best in other people and be positive about whatever situation we face. It gives us the energy to keep going in difficult circumstances, or while facing a seemingly impossible task. It's an attractive, infectious quality that draws others, whereas a negative attitude turns people away and means nothing new is ever attempted.

For example, when we have a pessimistic outlook, we can be so taken up with the problems and risks involved in a church program or outreach that we fail to take account of God's power—which can overcome everything. What's more, this attitude is also infectious: Your negativity, even if it's just expressed through a few cynical comments, can influence others.

What's the result? Their faith is weakened, they begin to lose enthusiasm for what God is doing in their neighborhood or city, and without enough support, the church program or outreach is undermined or even abandoned. Worse still, this can lead to long-term divisions within the church, seriously damaging the work of the Lord.

My friend, if this sounds uncomfortably close to home, let me challenge you to watch out for those unguarded comments and the urge to express your views. It can be right to be cautious before committing ourselves to a new project, but constant negativity is discouraging to others. Sometimes it may be better to keep your opinion to yourself!

Faith in Action

Of course, some of us are optimists by nature. We have a tendency to look on the bright side and hope for the best. In fact, some "optimists" are so focused on positive thinking that they refuse even to consider any negative aspects, as though it may be unlucky or give a bad impression. We don't want to be considered lacking in faith, after all!

But that is not the kind of optimism I mean, because that is merely burying our heads in the sand or insisting that something will come about if we want it enough. No, I'm talking about the kind of positive outlook that coolly weighs up a difficult situation and adds a hefty dose of faith to the mix. This kind of optimism is clear-sighted and realistic, yet full of faith in our all-powerful God. Instead of relying only on ourselves and how much we want to believe something, it puts our Heavenly Father right in the center of the situation and helps us move forward with Him.

Spiritual optimism is more than wishful thinking or hoping for the best. It's not about a three-year plan or ambitious self-seeking. It's even more than having confidence that everything will turn out all right. Instead, it is a clear choice to trust and believe in His promises as we learn more and more about Him and His grace toward us.

Optimism helps us overcome any difficulties or disappointments, because it lets us look back at what

Jesus has done for us and take this forward into the future. We know He loves us, and as His children we have nothing to fear, either in this life or the next. "For our citizenship is in heaven, from which we also eagerly wait for the Savior, the Lord Jesus Christ, who will transform our lowly body that it may be conformed to His glorious body…" (Philippians 3:20-21).

Until then, we are here to learn. Optimism helps us do that by giving us the opportunity to put our faith to work, discovering for ourselves just how real His promises are. Each time we do that, our faith becomes a little stronger. We are exercising our faith muscles!

Faith-Fueled Thinking

When Jesus fed the five thousand, the large crowd was hungry, and being in a remote area, there was nowhere for them to go and buy food. Jesus challenges the disciples to come up with a meal at short notice. We read that even eight months' wages wouldn't be enough for each person to have just one bite of food, even if there was anywhere to buy it! The disciples are stumped, and who can blame them?

But what happens next? In John's Gospel, a small boy comes forward and offers up his packed lunch (John 6:9). This generosity is both touching and ludicrous— you could call it a perfect example of spiritual optimism. As one of the disciples Andrew points out, how far would one child's picnic go among so many? Yet the boy has every faith in Jesus's ability to take this tiny offering and make it go round a huge crowd. Andrew, on the other hand, is thinking with his human brain and forgetting to take into account the supernatural power available to him in that situation.

We are not all great leaders, planners, or thinkers. Some of us find it difficult to think much at all, let alone think "outside the box"! I think most of us would admit defeat in that situation pretty quickly. That's fine, as long as we remember the power of Jesus to transform every question into an answer, and every problem into a solution. We don't have to come up with a carefully thought-out response or three-point plan every time we're stumped; we just have to offer the situation up to God before we get stumped! Make Him the first resort, not the last resort.

With this as our attitude, we will have the enthusiasm and motivation to press on. Despite any setbacks or suffering we face, we will know God's amazing strength and love as we dwell in Him. "Those who wait on the LORD shall renew their strength; they shall mount up with wings like eagles, they shall run and not be weary, they shall walk and not faint" (Isaiah 40:31).

Even if you have a natural tendency toward pessimism, your life can be filled with hope and joy through the Holy Spirit at work in you. This is spiritual optimism, which does not rely on our nature or feelings but on the powerful promises of our Father, who has said that He will never leave us or forsake us. He is truly in control, and nothing is too hard for Him.

WORKBOOK

Chapter 5 Questions

Question: Where does spiritual pessimism try to surface in your life? How can you convert it to optimism?

_____

_____

_____

_____

_____

_____

_____

_____

_____

_____

_____

Question: What are some joyful thoughts that can motivate you during your daily faith workouts?

_____

_____

_____

_____

_____

_____

_____

_____

_____

_____

_____

_____

_____

_____

Action: Maintain a spiritually optimistic outlook that translates into an active, joyful faith. Don't merely spout sunny platitudes, but focus on what God has done for you and what the Holy Spirit is doing in you. Let Him be your never-ending source of motivation to carry on.

Chapter 5 Notes

CHAPTER SIX

Use Them or Lose Them

Our faith muscles need to be exercised; if we don't use them, doubts will set in and our faith will be weakened. Use them or lose them!

Some of us, it is probably fair to say, have plenty of confidence. No one could accuse us of poor self-esteem! But it's vital to remember that God wants our confidence to be based on our faith in Him, not on our own abilities or strengths. If our confidence comes from ourselves, what will happen when we are faced with a situation we don't know how to deal with? What happens when self-confidence leads you astray?

Imagine that someone comes to you for counseling and guidance, and you advise them to act in a certain way—your way! You could make some serious mistakes through having too much faith in yourself.

We have already seen how faith leads to hope and optimism, because we believe and trust in the promises of God. Like the young man with the trust fund, we can also face the future with confidence—faith confidence—instead of fearing what might happen and wondering how we will cope with life's problems. We can rest assured that our Heavenly Father is in control of every area of our lives.

This sense of confidence will affect everything we do and feel. It not only influences how we see the future, but how we deal with the day to day issues we face now. Confidence also affects how we feel about ourselves and other people. It is not only about understanding God's love for us; it gives us a true sense of our identity as God's children, and it helps us remain strong when we are in danger of weakening in our faith.

That is because this confidence does not come from arrogance or a sense of pride; it is rooted in our acceptance of Jesus's sacrifice on our behalf and our belief in His resurrection, when He overcame the power of death once and for all. He is all-powerful, and nothing can snatch us out of His hand!

Overcoming the World

Let's look for a moment at the other side of the coin: a lack of confidence either in ourselves or in our Heavenly Father.

Lack of confidence is linked to issues of anxiety and poor self-esteem. Self-esteem refers to how we see ourselves, so poor self-esteem tends to focus on our own (possibly imagined) shortcomings, weaknesses, and failures, with an emphasis on what others think of us for falling short in some way.

Anxiety can be linked to self-esteem issues, but may also have nothing to do with what others are thinking. It is more about how we see the world around us, or uncertainty over what may happen in the future. Some of us worry quite a lot, especially when we are parents. Others only worry about the big things, like exams and medical tests, and are happy to ignore all the minor issues. But for some, a tendency to worry develops into a full-blown anxiety disorder that can be devastating, leaving sufferers unable to lead a normal life or even to leave the house.

Lack of confidence has to do with fear—fear of other people, fear of the future, fear of uncomfortable situations, fear of being afraid. For some of us it may be more of one thing than the other; it's possible to be comfortable about ourselves but still have anxiety issues in certain areas, for example. But while our attention is fixed either on ourselves, on other people's opinions, or on the possibility of something bad happening, our focus has moved away from our Heavenly Father and His love for us.

In 1 John 3:1 we read, "Behold what manner of love the Father has bestowed on us, that we should be called children of God!" He goes on to add, "For whatever is born of God overcomes the world. And this is the victory that has overcome the world—our faith. Who is he who overcomes the world, but he who believes that Jesus is the Son of God?" (1 John 5:4-5).

My friend, if you feel you are suffering from a lack of confidence, it may be time to think about the power available to you just for believing that Jesus is the Son of God. As John says, who else is able to overcome the whole world? Believing that Christ died for you is so powerful that you can overcome anything!

Despite this, we are sometimes hampered by our past or present circumstances, which can hold us back from being fully confident in God's love for us. Is there anything stopping you from moving forward in complete trust in our Heavenly Father? Do you have baggage in the form of bad habits, negative experiences, or painful memories of the past that you need to leave behind? Don't drag them along with you; you are a new creation in Christ! If you offer them up to Him, He will gladly shoulder your burden and leave you free to move on.

Faith Confidence, Not Self-Confidence

Those of us who don't have issues of poor self-esteem or anxiety may have trouble stepping out in faith. Used to having confidence in themselves, they may struggle to believe in God's promises or maintain confidence that He will act.

Self-confidence can also mean that we fail to notice or care for those with whom we come into contact, treating them brusquely because we are in a hurry or even completely ignoring them. Sadly, this is all too common in some churches, where we tend to follow routines and traditions, and often leave little room for others to join in.

One elderly lady hopefully offered every Christmas and Easter to help decorate the church. Each time her help was refused because "Jackie and Barbara always do it." Their vision for a beautifully decorated church was more important than showing love to a lonely older woman, and they had no intention of sharing the fun. Does your self-confidence mean you competently take charge of an activity because you do it so well? What happens to those who get in your way—do they end up crushed beneath the weight of your personality? Where is the love and humility in that?

No, our confidence must come from our identity as God's children, not from our own abilities. Self-confidence puts us on the throne and makes us answerable to no one. It is only one step away from pride. Remember, humility is not optional! If Jesus could wash his disciples' feet, and Peter and the other early church leaders could wait at tables, what does it mean for us? Clearly, humility is not merely something for our more modest brothers and sisters, but a vital character trait for all of us.

WORKBOOK

Chapter 6 Questions

Question: Do you tend to have too much self-confidence? How can you bring it in check?

_____

_____

_____

_____

_____

_____

_____

_____

_____

_____

_____

Question: Do you tend to have too little faith confidence? What burdens do you need to have the confidence to place on God's shoulders?

_____

_____

_____

_____

_____

_____

_____

_____

_____

_____

_____

_____

Action: Make faith in God—not in yourself—the bedrock of your confidence. Overcome your fears of life's dangers and uncertainty by moving forward with complete trust in God. Remember to stretch your faith muscles by sharing the burdens in your life with Him.

Chapter 6 Notes

CHAPTER SEVEN

To Boldly Go—One Step at a Time

In the Old Testament book of Daniel, King Nebuchadnezzar decreed that anyone who failed to bow down in worship to his golden image would be thrown into the burning fiery furnace. Shadrach, Meshach, and Abednego refused and would only worship the Lord. When threatened with being burned alive, this is what they answered:

> *...O Nebuchadnezzar, we have no need to answer you in this matter. If that is the case, our God whom we serve is able to deliver us from the burning fiery furnace, and He will deliver us from your hand, O king. But if not, let it be known to you, O king, that we do not serve your gods, nor will we worship the gold image which you have set up. — **Daniel 3:16-18***

These three men demonstrated complete faith in the Lord. They realized there was a strong possibility that they would be thrown into the furnace, but they knew God was able to save them. What they could be less sure of was whether He would choose to save them. Whatever the outcome, they trusted Him fully; He was still in control, even if they lost their lives.

God honored their faith and performed a miracle. King Nebuchadnezzar was amazed to see a fourth man "like the Son of God" walking about in the furnace with the others. Once released, Shadrach, Meshach, and Abednego were completely unharmed, with not even the smell of the fire on their clothes.

A wonderful example of boldness and faith—not only because of the deliverance God brought about, but because of the response of the three men. We may not always see Him in action, but our response in faith is more important than a miracle.

More than Conquerors

We have now looked at how our faith gives rise to hope, optimism, and confidence because of the promises of the One who said, "I will never leave you nor forsake you." Together, if we allow His power to work within us, these emotions we have been considering, which are based on the promises in God's word, produce a boldness that enables us to move outside our comfort zone and live the life God has in mind for us.

Boldness means being willing to step out in faith in whatever way we are led. It does not necessarily stem from a powerful sense of courage and self-assurance. Instead, even the most timid of people can demonstrate boldness once they make the decision to obey God in a difficult or threatening situation. In that case, the Holy Spirit will come to their aid and make them fearless and brave, just as He did for the early Christians who dared to risk their lives to speak out for Him.

In Acts 4, we read how, soon after Pentecost, Peter and John were hauled before the chief priests and elders and questioned about the healing of a crippled beggar. The apostles spoke out boldly, announcing the message of salvation through Jesus Christ to the same powerful group responsible for His death just a few weeks earlier.

We read that their elite audience was struck by their courage and authority, which were in stark contrast to their appearance and manner of speaking:

> *Now when they saw the boldness of Peter and John, and perceived that they were uneducated and untrained men, they marveled. And they realized that they had been with Jesus. — Acts 4:13*

The bravery of the apostles was a clear indication of their personal relationship with Jesus; they were becoming like Him.

Peter and John were threatened with further action if they continued speaking about Jesus, and then released. They reported back to the other believers, and the whole church was united in prayer. What did they pray for—protection? No, boldness! "Now, Lord, look on their threats, and grant to Your servants that with all boldness they may speak Your word" (Acts 4:29).

A Syrian Christian recently visited a few European churches to share how the church in Syria was coping in the appalling conditions resulting from the long-running civil war. He was raising awareness, but would soon be returning home despite the danger. There was no doubt in his mind that he was needed there, and he asked for prayer—not for his safety, but for boldness.

In Romans 8, Paul talks about God's overwhelming love for His children and the strength it gives him to continue his mission:

> *Who shall separate us from the love of Christ? Shall tribulation, or distress, or persecution, or famine, or nakedness, or peril, or sword? As it is written: "For Your sake we are killed all day long; we are accounted as sheep for the slaughter." Yet in all these things we are more than conquerors through Him who loved us. For I am persuaded that neither death nor life, nor angels nor principalities nor powers, nor things present nor things to come, nor height nor depth, nor any other created thing, shall be able to separate us from the love of God which is in Christ Jesus our Lord. — **Romans 8:35-39**

Isn't that amazing? More than conquerors!

God in Control

Being bold is about taking our faith and seeing what God can do with it. With Him beside us, we don't need to be frightened about what might happen. Instead of focusing on what others might do or think, we can concentrate on Him and move ahead in the strength He provides.

When we focus only on our weaknesses and fears, we can easily slip into spiritual apathy and even cowardice. We are overlooking His love at work in us, which has the power to transform us completely. Our faith is stunted all the time. Our outlook remains one of negativity and discouragement, and this in turn communicates itself to other people. If you feel this could be your attitude, ask God to show you how He can change everything!

A church that is made up of Christians who lack spiritual boldness is a church that is failing in the work of the Lord. That's why it is so important for individuals to avoid spreading negativity by seeking forgiveness and renewal from our Heavenly Father. He is always ready to bring healing where there is hurt, so don't let your past fears or negative experiences cast a long shadow over your future in Him.

That's not to say, of course, that we will no longer be hurt or upset—of course we will. Building relationships, sharing with others, trying to help those in need, and growing as Christians will all make us vulnerable. Being bold means taking that risk, weighing up the consequences, and going ahead anyway, knowing that our Heavenly Father is in charge and will continue to bring healing and peace.

Boldness or Bullying?

Exercising faith is not about what we can do, but about what the Lord is directing us to do in His strength. God said to Paul, "My strength is made perfect in weakness" (2 Corinthians 12:9). Accordingly, Paul wrote, "I can do all things through Christ who strengthens me" (Philippians 4:13).

If you feel you are lacking boldness, it is time to seize hold of His promises and witness how His strength will be made perfect through your weakness. John says, "There is no fear in love; but perfect love casts out fear…he who fears has not been made perfect in love" (1 John 4:18). If you are habitually negative and timid, ask God to remind you of His perfect love that casts out all our human anxieties, painful memories, and bad experiences.

However, if you have a tendency to be strong and outspoken, take care to temper your boldness with meekness, love, and patience. Spiritual boldness does not bully people into going along with your ideas, bearing all before you and wiping out any opposition to your plans.

It does not make others feel small for not being as courageous as you. It seeks to uplift and strengthen, but always in a spirit of love for others. And it puts God first and foremost, seeking His will above all, because it's no use being bold when you are mistaken.

If your motivation is not one hundred percent right, if you are secretly seeking your own glory instead of God's, your boldness will only land you in a burning fiery furnace of your own making!

Wherever you are on this journey, take it one step at a time and see how He will use you, if you are willing and humble.

WORKBOOK

Chapter 7 Questions

Question: What is a challenging situation in which you've balked at doing the right thing or following God's leading because of the apparent consequences? What did you decide, and how did the situation turn out?

_____
_____
_____
_____
_____
_____
_____
_____
_____
_____
_____
_____

Question: When have you experienced or observed boldness that became bullying? How can you make sure your boldness doesn't turn into bullying?

_____

_____

_____

_____

_____

_____

_____

_____

_____

_____

_____

_____

Action: Have the boldness to step out in faith according to God's leading, no matter the apparent consequences.

See what God can accomplish in you when you don't get in the way! Allow His love to transform you and propel you forward. At the same time, temper your boldness with meekness, love, and patience so that it doesn't translate into bullying.

Chapter 7 Notes

CHAPTER EIGHT

Giving Faith a Workout

So you're a Christian. Wonderful! Everything will be sweetness and light from here on in—or will it?

Some well-meaning people imply that once you become a Christian by repenting and accepting Jesus's sacrifice on your behalf, you will never experience any further problems or difficulties. You won't be taunted, bullied, mugged, or beaten up. You won't have days where you shout at the kids, burn the dinner, and fight with your husband or wife. You will never suffer sickness, be made redundant, lose all your money or your home, or watch a loved one die.

My friend, if that's what you believe, then you should know that being a Christian is not an easy way out. It's a popular belief in certain quarters that Christians need a crutch to help them get through the difficulties of life, but let me tell you: If you are looking for an easy ride, you've come to the wrong place.

Any pastor will tell you that bad things can happen to Christians, the same as they do for anyone else. Yes, our Heavenly Father protects us from many dangers—we will never even know the full extent of His care and protection—and of course He is with us whatever happens. However, we are still real people living in the real world and exposed to many of the same problems and difficulties as anyone else.

If becoming a Christian was a guarantee of a charmed existence where nothing ever went wrong, the world would be full of so-called Christians all living a long, easy life! But Jesus never promised a pleasant or comfortable ride. In fact, sometimes being a Christian might make it worse. In our twenty–first-century society, Christians experience taunts, discrimination, and lawsuits in some parts of the Western world, and hate crimes, persecution, imprisonment, and even death in other countries.

So what did Jesus say to His disciples? He didn't assure them, "Don't worry, everything's going to be fine." Instead, He told them the truth: "In the world you will have tribulation; but be of good cheer, I have overcome the world" (John 16:33). Although we face these problems, we don't need to fear them or get depressed, because He is with us every day and He has overcome much greater dangers than those facing us.

Learning Perseverance

According to Webster's dictionary, *perseverance* is defined as "to persist in an idea, purpose, or task despite obstacles." It's easy to see how this applies to our journey into faith. Don't give up because things are getting tough! When your prayers seem to go unheard and you don't sense the reassurance of His presence near you, that changes nothing—He is still there. If one of you has moved away, it isn't Him!

What does the Bible say about tribulation? You may be surprised to learn that Paul doesn't regard it as something unpleasant yet unavoidable, like going to the dentist or filling in your tax return. In fact, he welcomes the many difficulties and dangers that crowd in on him at every turn—threats, violence, imprisonment, plots to kill him, even shipwreck and snake bites! His attitude is far more positive than either yours or mine would be in those circumstances.

In his letter to the Romans, as we saw in an earlier chapter, Paul says, "we also glory in tribulations, knowing that tribulation produces perseverance; and perseverance, character; and character, hope" (Romans 5:3-4). So persevering in faith through the hard times is part of our growth as God's children. We are exercising our faith muscles.

What happens after that? Paul goes on to say, "Now hope does not disappoint, because the love of God has been poured out in our hearts by the Holy Spirit who was given to us" (Romans 5:5). God's love is real, and even if we don't sense Him near us, we can be assured He won't be far away!

Those of us who are parents know all too well how it feels when our baby is old enough to start school. We can't follow them in there; we have to let them go as part of the next stage of their life. That doesn't mean we stop caring about them! Instead, we think of them most of the day and look forward to giving them a big hug once school is over. Of course God can and does stay with them all day, even when our little angels decide they are too big for hugs. God's love never fails.

So whatever you may face, our Heavenly Father will be there beside you. There is a wonderful verse in Deuteronomy that tells us, "The Eternal God is your refuge, and underneath are the everlasting arms..." (Deuteronomy 33:27). With this promise to lean on, we have strength to keep on exercising those faith muscles and to persevere through our doubts and difficulties.

Through the Valley of the Shadow

Unfortunately, no life on this earth is untouched by suffering. Some people see more than their fair share, while others seem to have a relatively carefree existence.

We don't know why this is, or even why God allows it. There are numerous questions that must remain unanswered for now, but many painful and distressing situations can be recognized as resulting from man's sinful nature.

Other tragic circumstances seem to have nothing to do with sin or pride; they appear to be completely random, and these cases are even harder to bear. "Where is God in all this?" people wonder. The answer is that He is right there with us as we go through adversity. It is certainly not His will for anyone to suffer, although you may sometimes hear people say that it is. In fact, Jesus went out of His way to relieve pain and cure disease, instead of walking away and saying, "I guess that's the result of sin for you!"

The Bible warns us many times to expect tribulation and suffering. Being warned means we can prepare ourselves, through God's grace, to face whatever lies ahead. If we are truly making every effort to walk with God every day, in His strength and grace, suffering will not diminish our faith; in fact, it will strengthen it.

The much-loved Psalm 23 describes the blessings of knowing God as our shepherd. The first part speaks of the comfort and joys of peaceful growth:

The LORD is my shepherd; I shall not want. He makes me to lie down in green pastures; He leads me beside the still waters. He restores my soul; He leads me in

the paths of righteousness for His name's sake. —
Psalm 23:1-3

In the second part, the times of restoration and peace have vanished. Instead, David speaks of the harsh experience of suffering and danger, but still has the sense of God's presence:

*Yea, though I walk through the valley of the shadow of death, I will fear no evil; for You are with me; Your rod and Your staff, they comfort me. — **Psalm 23:4***

Likewise, Isaiah admonishes us:

*Who among you fears the LORD? Who obeys the voice of His Servant? Who walks in darkness and has no light? Let him trust in the name of the LORD and rely upon his God. — **Isaiah 50:10***

In the valley of the shadow, God is still there and He is still our shepherd, it's just that we may not notice the blessings of His presence until we climb out of the valley and look back. Then we realize He didn't abandon us; He was there with us, still leading and guiding, still teaching us to follow Him.

WORKBOOK

Chapter 8 Questions

Question: In what ways does life seem more difficult as a Christian? In what ways does a faith-filled life seem easier than one without faith?

_____

_____

_____

_____

_____

_____

_____

_____

_____

_____

_____

Question: How do you know God is with you in times of tribulation? How has He comforted you during difficult times in the past?

_____
_____
_____
_____
_____
_____
_____
_____
_____
_____
_____

Action: Don't expect an easy ride just because you're a faith-filled Christian. In fact, expect the same suffering and trials that other people experience—and sometimes more. Yet never forget that God is right beside you every step of the way.

Chapter 8 Notes

_____

_____

_____

_____

_____

_____

_____

_____

_____

_____

_____

_____

_____

_____

_____

_____

_____

_____

_____

_____

_____

_____

_____

_____

_____

CHAPTER NINE

From Zero to Hero

Maybe you have found out that, in the face of problems and opposition, your faith isn't as strong as you thought. If you are experiencing doubts and fears, you will be relieved to hear that the Bible is full of people called by God who were pretty weak. In many cases they went on to become great leaders, prophets, or teachers—so don't despair!

In the last chapter we looked at how, as Christians, we are called to persevere when things get tough. Even though we face problems and hardship, and may even walk through "the valley of the shadow of death," we know God's love and faithfulness are always there, supporting us and giving us strength.

Let's take a look at a few of these unlikely heroes.

Face to Face with God

Moses was a Hebrew child adopted by Pharaoh's daughter and brought up in the Egyptian royal court. He grew up with some identity issues and a short temper. One day, he murdered an Egyptian who was beating a Hebrew man, and ran away when he realized his secret was known. He ended up working as a shepherd, a safe and unthreatening job in an area where no one knew him. Then one day he saw a burning bush in the desert that, although ablaze, did not burn up. God spoke to him from within the bush and turned his life around. "I will send you to Pharaoh that you may bring My people, the children of Israel, out of Egypt" (Exodus 3:10).

You might think that, in view of his past, Moses would be highly motivated to rescue his people from their status as slaves. But he put up quite a struggle, even though God told him that those who wanted to kill him in revenge for the murder were now dead and he could safely go back to Egypt. In fact, Moses came up with four different arguments for not doing it. God even showed him two miraculous signs to boost his courage, but Moses was having none of it. "O Lord, please send someone else to do it," he says (Exodus 4:13).

Not exactly willing, then, but in the end Moses obeyed, along with his brother Aaron as support. Exodus details the difficulties and struggles they had with the Pharaoh and even with the Israelites, who saw their tough conditions getting worse. However, when you read through the account of the ten plagues, it is striking to see how Moses's relationship with the Lord developed: praying, hearing His voice, gaining confidence, and seeing miraculous signs and wonders every day.

This increased even more during the years that followed the exodus from Egypt. Moses would spend hours meeting with the Lord; his face would glow so much afterward that he took to wearing a veil. He was the man who received the Ten Commandments and the whole of God's Covenant with the Israelites. In fact, we read that "the LORD spoke to Moses face to face, as a man speaks to his friend" (Exodus 33:11).

Asking for Signs

Judges 6 introduces us to Gideon at a time when the country was under attack from the Midianites. The Angel of the Lord appears to him and says, "The LORD is with you, you mighty man of valor!" (Judges 6:12). We see that Gideon doesn't question the description, even though he is threshing wheat inside a winepress to conceal it from the enemy—resourceful, but hardly the actions of a superhero. Maybe he doesn't argue about that because he secretly sees himself as a courageous warrior! Instead, he immediately starts arguing about the first part and wonders why bad things are happening if the Lord is with the Israelites (Judges 6:13).

Unlike Moses, Gideon takes very little time to be convinced that he has a part to play. "Go in this might of yours, and you shall save Israel from the hand of the Midianites. Have I not sent you?" the Lord says (Judges 6:14). Gideon seems to agree pretty readily. On the other hand, he starts to have doubts once he gets his battle orders. Whereas Moses was shown two miraculous signs before reluctantly giving in to God's calling, Gideon asks for them before going into battle. It seems the mighty warrior is less brave than he thought.

For the first sign, he spreads out a sheep's fleece and prays for the dew to fall only on the fleece, not on the ground around it:

> *If there is dew on the fleece only, and it is dry on all the ground, then I shall know that You will save Israel by my hand, as You have said.* — ***Judges 6:37***

The next day, the ground is dry while the fleece is soaking wet. Gideon isn't convinced, though, and this time asks for the reverse to happen.

> *"Let me test, I pray, just once more with the fleece; let it now be dry only on the fleece, but on all the ground let there be dew." And God did so that night. It was dry on the fleece only, but there was dew on all the ground.* — ***Judges 6:39-40***

The story of Gideon's fleece still inspires Christians today when they are seeking guidance, or believe God may be calling them to do something extraordinary. We may not use sheepskin, but we can still ask Him to demonstrate His will. If you are going to set a "fleece," don't make it be too easy! It's got to be something pretty unlikely so that you can be one hundred percent sure. One woman I knew asked for a certain word to be said on the evening news show. When she heard the word she immediately knew the Lord was speaking to her.

God has another surprise in store for Gideon. He tells him that he has too many men! Setting a series of filters, the army is whittled down from thirty-two thousand to just three hundred, who win a great victory through clever tactics. Perhaps the Lord knew that His mighty man of valor might be tempted to boast in his own strength and skill if he won at the head of a large army. Instead, all the glory belongs to God.

Flawed but Faithful

We are familiar with the story of the young David, overcoming the giant Goliath with his homemade weapons and becoming king of Israel after many years of hardship and danger. We sometimes forget, however, about his midlife crisis and the series of disastrous events that followed.

In 2 Samuel 11, we read the story of David and Bathsheba, a sad but not uncommon story of adultery. Instead of going off to war as usual, David sent the army off under his second in command, Joab, while he loitered at home. It wasn't long before he noticed (surely not for the first time) a neighbor, a beautiful woman bathing in full view of the palace, and they started an affair. She falls pregnant and David embarks on a series of attempts to get her husband Uriah home from the army to sleep with his wife. When that fails, he orders Joab to place Uriah in the midst of the fighting and then withdraw support so that he is killed, and that is what happens.

Psalm 51 was written by David after this event. It clearly shows his distress and repentance, and his trust in God's unfailing love despite his sin. His prayer, "Create in me a pure heart, O God" (Psalm 51:10), has been echoed through the ages ever since.

David is a key figure in the Old Testament; in fact, Jesus is called the Son of David, as his earthly father Joseph was a direct descendant. It may seem strange the brave and God-fearing slayer of Goliath and many other enemies, the writer of so many psalms, would fall so low. It might seem even stranger that God would choose someone who was capable of making such a serious mistake, an adulterer and murderer, to be king of Israel and part of the family tree, but He knows all our weaknesses and loves us anyway.

In fact, our Father delights in using weaker, flawed people like these men—and of course, in Gideon's case, He had to make Gideon even weaker before He could use him.

Faith Beyond Failure

What about the New Testament? Almost all the disciples were also simple, uneducated men. After three years of living with Jesus, with all the opportunities they had for learning about Him firsthand, not only did they fail to understand a lot of His teachings but they all abandoned Him at the time of His arrest. As we know, Peter even denied any knowledge of Him—not once but three times!

Yet despite such a massive failure, God hadn't finished with Peter and the remaining ten disciples. Once the Holy Spirit had come upon them after Jesus's resurrection, they were transformed into mighty evangelists, preachers, and healers, who witnessed God's power at work through them. Peter especially became one of the key leaders of the first-century church, speaking to powerful leaders and large crowds with great authority and conviction.

If you are burdened with a sense of failure as a Christian, you may want to follow Peter's advice:

Humble yourselves under the mighty hand of God, that He may exalt you in due time, casting all your care upon Him, for He cares for you. — *1 Peter 5:6-7*

WORKBOOK

Chapter 9 Questions

Question: When have you "set a sheepskin," figuratively speaking, to try to understand God's will for you? How did the situation turn out?

_____

_____

_____

_____

_____

_____

_____

_____

_____

_____

_____

Question: In what ways do you see yourself as similar to any one (or more) of the flawed biblical heroes discussed in this chapter? What faith lessons can you draw from their experience?

_____

_____

_____

_____

_____

_____

_____

_____

_____

_____

_____

_____

Action: When problems surround you or you experience a temporary setback, remember heroes of the faith like Moses, Gideon, David, and Peter who resisted God's leading and slipped up big-time. Take courage and keep pressing forward in faith!

Chapter 9 Notes

CHAPTER TEN

Tuning In to God

When we get off our spiritual couch and begin to exercise our faith muscles, we start to become more familiar with the way God speaks to us, guides us, and leads us to do His will. Discerning His voice, however, doesn't always come easily.

I once heard of a youth pastor in another church who happily devoted every evening and weekend to his ministry, completely overlooking the needs of his young wife, who hardly ever saw him. In the end, she issued an ultimatum: It's me or the job! He was forced to acknowledge that his youth work had become so important to him that it had become his only focus. It had become *his* work, rather than God's. The realization had almost come too late; to save their marriage, he and his wife left the area and started afresh somewhere else.

It is good to wholeheartedly serve the Lord, but we need to allow time for others, too. That's partly because we need the support and love of our spouses and families, even though they may have their failings! It is also easy to get so involved in church activities that we neglect the people around us, which is not a good witness to them of God's care. Serving the Lord doesn't only mean being busy with church matters; we can also serve Him by showing love and encouragement to our families and friends.

Sometimes it is very hard to hear what God is saying to us. His guidance can get confused in our minds with what we want, or what other people would like us to do. We might see ourselves in a certain role that is not what God has in mind for us. We might also be influenced by other factors. For example, the needs and wishes of our spouse or our parents are important too.

So, in the face of so many pressures and demands on our time, how can we learn to discern God's voice? Let's look at how He spoke to two different people in the Bible.

Changing Direction

Most of us are familiar with the story in Acts 9 of the conversion of Saul. As a young man, he zealously pursued the new Christian Church, which, he believed, was a blasphemous sect; he would arrest men and women, and even supervise their death by stoning. On his way to Damascus one day, he and the men with him saw a flash of bright light. Saul fell to the ground, unable to see. They all heard a voice saying, "Saul, Saul, why are you persecuting me?" He asked, "Who are you, Lord?" The voice replied, "I am Jesus, whom you are persecuting" (Acts 9:4-5).

After this dramatic event, followed by three days of blindness, Saul was baptized into the same church he had been pursuing so fanatically. At some stage he changed his name to Paul and went on to become a bold and fearless evangelist, spreading the word through many different countries and planting churches wherever he went. He spent years in prison for his faith and wrote constantly to various churches and coworkers to teach and encourage them. Many of these letters were preserved; about half of the books in our New Testament are letters from Paul.

What an amazing story! Only God could reach such a man and transform him into a powerful tool He could use for His glory. Saul clearly needed this kind of approach, as nothing less would have stopped him in his tracks—literally—and turned him in the right direction. Yet we do not often hear the voice of Jesus so clearly and dramatically.

The Still, Small Voice

In 1 Kings 19 we find Elijah, whose story is a complete contrast to Paul's. He was a prophet who served God tirelessly, often in very dangerous circumstances, and there are many examples given of God's miraculous interventions in answer to Elijah's prayers. But one day, faced with a death threat from the wicked queen Jezebel, Elijah finds circumstances to be too much and he runs away. He sits in the shade of a small tree in the desert and prays for death (1 Kings 19:1-4).

Exhausted and discouraged, he lies down and falls asleep—only to be woken by an angel offering food and water. This happens twice, and then he is strong enough to continue his journey (1 Kings 19:5-8).

Once he is safely hidden, resting in a cave, the Lord asks him, "What are you doing here, Elijah?" Elijah lists all his activities and his fear that his life is in danger. He thinks he is the only prophet left in Israel, as all the others have been killed, so there is a sense of responsibility as well as fear. But this isn't really an answer to God's question (1 Kings 19: 9-10)!

The Lord makes him stand outside on the mountain and watch for His presence. What does Elijah see? Firstly, a mighty wind; secondly, an earthquake; thirdly, a fire. All powerful and majestic events, but we are told the Lord was not in any of them. Where was He (1 Kings 19:11-12)?

After the fire comes a still, small voice, and it is this small voice that tells Elijah what he must do, and that helps him see things through God's eyes. For a start, there are still seven thousand people in Israel who have remained faithful to the Lord. What's more, one of the things Elijah is required to do is appoint a certain man, Elisha, to be his assistant and eventually succeed him as God's prophet (1 Kings 19:12-18).

Of course, we don't always hear actual words; sometimes it may be a strong sense or feeling, for example. But this story demonstrates how God often speaks in the stillness, not the bluster and drama. He waits until He has our full attention and won't compete with anyone. It is also noteworthy that the Lord provides for all the needs of His servant: food, water, rest, shelter, and support. He knows when things are getting too much for us.

When Things Go Wrong

Despite listening for God's voice, we sometimes get it wrong. It is all too easy to get frustrated when things do not go as we planned or within our perceived timeframe, and then we may either give up or begin to neglect our responsibilities to God and to others. Our eyes leave Jesus and just focus inward. Sometimes we blame ourselves for what has or hasn't happened. We might say, "It's my fault—I can never get anything right. I'm not spiritual enough. I should have spent more time in prayer, or not been so proud and ignored other people's views." Of course, all that could be true, but sometimes we beat ourselves up unnecessarily.

Worse, and more commonly, we seek someone else to blame! "If only so-and-so had come through a bit faster. If only they'd worked harder or been more dedicated." Before long, we've managed to convince ourselves that when things don't work out as we intended, the blame lies entirely with someone else.

Yes, there are times when, despite asking God for guidance and listening for His voice, we seem to be facing a brick wall. Everything we try seems to be in vain and no doors open to allow us to proceed. But this can be a sign of God's leading; if you have taken the wrong path, coming to a dead end is one way of showing you that you have strayed from His plan.

One of the first things He says to Elijah after his crisis is "Go back the way you came" (1 Kings 19:15 NIV). In Isaiah we read, "Your ears shall hear a word behind you, saying, 'This is the way, walk in it,' whenever you turn to the right hand or whenever you turn to the left" (Isaiah 30:21).

A woman had been offered a job in another city, but was having trouble finding somewhere to live. After searching for some time, she found an apartment in an area she liked, but the realtor failed to meet her as agreed. In fact, an investigation revealed the appointment had not even been entered in the diary and the property had since been rented out to another tenant. The woman began to question whether she should take the job after all, knowing that God always opens and closes the doors at the right time. She started looking elsewhere and found all the arrangements for work and a home fell into place.

Even when we don't see the way ahead, we are called to persevere in our faith and in the tasks we have been given. Once you are certain of His guiding, the only doubt can be over His timeframe! If the Lord has laid something on your heart, it is not for you to know the when or the how. It's just a case of being faithful until the time is right. That is true faith: Faith that trusts and believes without having a wealth of detailed information to draw upon.

WORKBOOK

Chapter 10 Questions

Question: When was a time that you heard God's still, small voice? How did you respond? What happened?

_____

_____

_____

_____

_____

_____

_____

_____

_____

_____

_____

_____

Question: What specifically can you do every day to make it easier to hear God's voice?

_____

_____

_____

_____

_____

_____

_____

_____

_____

_____

_____

_____

_____

Action: Practice listening to God so you can discern His will for you throughout your day, whether His voice comes as a boom or a whisper. And when you hit a brick wall in life, tune in to God—then turn around!

Chapter 10 Notes

_____
_____
_____
_____
_____
_____
_____
_____
_____
_____
_____
_____
_____
_____
_____
_____
_____
_____
_____
_____
_____
_____
_____
_____
_____

CHAPTER ELEVEN

Exercising Those Faith Muscles

One day, a secretary whose job involved a great deal of typing began to experience pain in her elbows. At first, she made a few adjustments to her chair and posture to try to make things more comfortable. When that didn't work, she went to an osteopath. As soon as he examined her shoulders, back, and neck, he could see the cause of the pain. He told her, "Your muscles have taken a vacation!" Her fingers and hands were getting plenty of exercise thanks to the typing, but because her shoulders were much less active, those muscles were weak, giving rise to all kinds of problems.

For this reason, people who want to start building up their fitness levels are recommended to take professional advice. It may be tempting to avoid the public embarrassment of the gym and set out to get fit in private, but exercising and building muscles at random puts you at risk of injury. It's much better to have a proper, well-designed exercise program.

So far we have been looking at the ways our faith in God's love and forgiveness can impact our lives. We have seen how it gives rise to hope, optimism, and boldness. We know about the need to persevere when things get tough so that God can work through us despite our faults and failings.

But like the secretary's shoulders, and all of our muscles, our faith muscles need regular exercise to prevent them from wasting away. If they are weak, they need building up. Faith doesn't just appear overnight; it has to be cultivated through a faith workout program tailored to our personal needs.

A Personalized Training Program

Did you know that, as a Christian, you have a personal coach who knows all your strengths and weaknesses? The Holy Spirit is your counselor and guide, and He will lead you through your own personalized training program. Some people learn fast, others more slowly; a valuable lesson for one person is unnecessary for another, and so on. We are all different, and God treats us all as individuals.

Before David became king of Israel—and experienced his midlife crisis—he spent his youth as a shepherd. The youngest in the family and alone on the hills all day, he learned how to defend himself and his flock against hungry predators using just a homemade sling. This was David's training program; most importantly, alongside the physical skills, he learned to trust God to keep him safe. By the time he fought Goliath, he had already killed lions and bears, and had developed a deep personal relationship with God. No wonder he tells Saul, "The LORD, who delivered me from the paw of the lion and from the paw of the bear, He will deliver me from the hand of this Philistine" (1 Samuel 17:37).

You may not have had the same training program as David, but none of your life experiences have been pointless. You might feel that you haven't gained much from them, or even that they have only damaged you, but God uses all the things we have been through to develop our faith as we walk with Him. Sometimes it is only after we look back that we realize how He was teaching and preparing us in advance for whatever He had in mind for us.

Getting to Know Your Coach

In an earlier chapter, I mentioned the story of Bryan, who as a child had prayed for his grandmother when she became sick. When the old lady died, Bryan blamed God. This is a common reaction when bad things happen, but that kind of prayer is like expecting a costly Christmas present from someone you haven't spoken to all year—it's much better to build up a relationship first!

If we want to exercise our faith muscles, we need to be consistent. We need to spend time with our head coach and personal trainer in the faith—our Heavenly Father and His Holy Spirit—both alone and in fellowship with our brothers and sisters in the Church. We have to build up our relationship as His children, and make sure He is our focus and our motivation in everything we do.

Sometimes that can be difficult, especially in a church situation where our motives can be unclear, even to ourselves. For example, we might like the idea of healing the sick. We wonder if maybe we have the gift of healing—that would be so cool! In unguarded moments, we might even begin to picture a growing ministry, a bestselling book, even a TV show! Well, we may indeed have the gift of healing, but this kind of thinking puts us at center stage instead of God. The gift of healing, like so many other things, comes from Him to bless other people, and not from ourselves or for ourselves. Our focus has to be on Jesus.

Building Layers of Trust

We also need to learn to trust God in the small things before we can ask Him for the big ones. Sadly, many people in our churches every Sunday do not even think of asking for His help on a day to day basis. Our Heavenly Father wants to be part of every aspect of our lives. I know people who have cried out to God for a sick dog, a computer having a meltdown, or even when something has gone missing that they need to find, and He has provided an answer every time.

A friend of mine injured his toe and blood was trapped under the nail. The pressure was agonizing until he was able to visit his doctor, who melted a hole through the toenail and released the blood. The doctor explained that nails are made up of keratin, the same as hair. Instead of growing in long strands, however, nails grow in layers, in depth as well as length, which is why they are so strong.

This is how our faith needs to grow, too. It stems from our relationship with our Heavenly Father and is built up, layer upon layer. Every time you learn a little more about the Lord and what He can do for you, you are adding another layer to your level of trust. This makes for a strong, stable foundation that remains firm, even when something bad happens.

Jumping Spiritual Hurdles

When we have consistency and trust in a relationship, we begin to build up experience over time. We know how the other person feels about things, the way they behave in certain situations, and how far we can trust them. In the same way, over the months and years of our walk with God, we learn to have more confidence in Him and more understanding of ourselves. When something bad happens to us, we know how to get through it with His help, instead of going into a spiritual meltdown and losing our faith at the first hurdle.

If someone has a chronic medical condition, they learn over the years how to deal with the problem. It may still be horrible, but they know how to cope. They learn to recognize the signs of a flare-up and what to do to alleviate them. If your car has had problems in the past, you know what to do when the same thing starts to happen again. In the same way, when we get used to walking with God, our experience of His faithfulness helps us to trust Him more—just like David—knowing He is with us in the good times and the bad.

Sometimes you may see an ad for a small business— say, a local builder—that reads, "No job too big or too small!" Next time you see that, I hope it reminds you of the whole range of things God can do in your life. Don't leave Him on the sideline or feel He has better things to do! Like any loving parent, He wants to be involved and help you build up those layers of trust as you move ahead in faith.

WORKBOOK

Chapter 11 Questions

Question: What spiritual strengths or gifts do you have? How has God used these strengths, or how might He use them?

_____

_____

_____

_____

_____

_____

_____

_____

_____

_____

_____

Question: What personal weaknesses must you account for as you walk with God through daily life? How does the Holy Spirit help you jump these spiritual hurdles, or how can you let Him help you?

_____
_____
_____
_____
_____
_____
_____
_____
_____
_____
_____
_____

Action: Remember that God has a personalized training program for each of us. As you spend time getting to know His Holy Spirit, your personal trainer, learn to practice your faith by trusting God in small things first. Then, the more you grow and adapt to your spiritual training regimen, the bigger the hurdles you can jump!

Chapter 11 Notes

CHAPTER TWELVE

Practicing Faith

Do your friends and neighbors know you are a Christian? Could a stranger figure it out just by observing you for a few hours?

An elderly woman was recently asked about her faith and, in particular, about any answers to prayer she would like to share. She pursed up her lips and said it was too private and solemn a matter to talk about. She was a dedicated church member, although sadly her concept of living a Christian life was long on devotions but rather short on humor and tolerance.

Is that what it means to live by faith? No, I'm talking about the kind of lifestyle that is completely transformed by faith: A vibrant faith that attracts, not repels, other people. Faith like that can change your life and take you to some surprising places.

I'm not talking about someone saying "Praise the Lord!" every few minutes—although that's a great thing to do. Nor am I talking about the religious kind of person who takes life, and the outward forms of Christianity, very seriously. As we know, going to church doesn't make you a Christian any more than going to the supermarket makes you a can of beans. It's about a personal relationship, not a set of rules.

Throughout this book, we have been considering what it means to have faith and how we can exercise that faith to grow in our relationship with our Heavenly Father. We've looked at hope, boldness, and faithfulness, at how we can learn to discern His guidance and what to do when things go wrong. And we've seen how some of the greatest figures in the Bible made mistakes and had their failings, just like us.

Now we're going to think about how we put our faith into practice in our daily lives.

No Guarantees

Hebrews 11 gives us a long list of Old Testament characters who lived a life of faith. Some of them we have already looked at, like Moses, Gideon, and David, and we know that they weren't perfect. Abraham too had his failings, but his faith shone like a beacon:

> *By faith Abraham obeyed when he was called to go out to the place which he would receive as an inheritance. And he went out, not knowing where he was going. By faith he dwelt in the land of promise as*

in a foreign country, dwelling in tents with Isaac and Jacob, the heirs with him of the same promise; for he waited for the city which has foundations, whose builder and maker is God. — **Hebrews 11:8-10**

Abraham obeyed God's call and left his comfortable situation in the city of Ur. He set out for the Promised Land, which God said He would give to him and his descendants as their inheritance. He had no idea where he was going, and once he got there he and his family spent the rest of their lives living in tents—a nomadic existence with no sense of stability or permanence.

The first lesson we can learn from Abraham is that when we accept God's call, or obey His Word, we have no guaranteed outcome. We don't know where it will take us. Sometimes it seems to make no sense. One Christian speaker received an invitation to visit a church in Barbados, and he believed God was prompting him to go—even though there were only ten people present to hear him speak. Because of his obedience, doors were opened that night that would have remained firmly closed if he had decided it was a waste of time.

Living by faith means we follow where God leads us, regardless of the consequences. We have to leave those to Him. Like Abraham, we may never even see the results of our actions. We just go with God.

That means, for some people at least, there must be doubt and a sense of failure; you may feel you have stepped out in obedience only for everything to come unstuck. No doubt Abraham, and many other people in the Bible, also wondered where they went wrong. But we are only responsible for our response, not for the consequences. God will take care of all those.

Holding Out for the Promises

Sometimes we all have a tendency to behave like children, as I'm sure you will agree! This can be good for our walk with God in some respects, as children are generally trusting, but mostly it is rather negative. In this instance, we are often like kids in the way we perceive time. We expect everything to happen right now, not unlike a child who protests, "I want it now!" and asks, "Are we there yet?"

The second lesson we learn from Abraham is that God doesn't work to our timeframe. In fact, He operates outside of time as we know it. Like the old hymn says, "A thousand ages in Thy sight are like an evening gone."[4] If He has promised something, it will happen, but not necessarily in our lifetime. As with Abraham, part of living by faith is waiting for the promises to be fulfilled. That means living in full expectation, not forgetting about them or losing hope.

In the end, a couple of centuries later, God's word to Abraham and his descendants was fulfilled, and the people of Israel inherited the land He had promised.

Focusing on the Finish Line

During all the time Abraham waited for the promise, he and his family lived in tents. It must have been hard at times to look back and compare his old life with his new one, but he knew God was faithful. Hebrews 11:10 tells us that "he waited for the city which has foundations, whose builder and maker is God."

Abraham spent more of his time looking forward than backward, and his focus was on a heavenly city, not the walls of his tent. So the third lesson we need to learn is to keep our minds and thoughts on what God is building, both here on earth and more importantly in heaven. Because of Jesus's death and resurrection, we know we will one day be with Him, and that is our true reality.

Whatever God calls us to do, or wherever we live, we are likely to face disappointments and disillusionment. Nothing is ever one hundred percent perfect—or not for long! But having a long-term view of life helps us keep things in perspective, and we are less likely to be troubled by setbacks.

I recently heard of a man studying at a famous Bible college who felt he was called to be a pastor. Everything was going well until he discovered that while he was away at college, his wife was having an affair. Sad to say, this news shattered the man's faith. Not only did he drop out of college, but he also decided that God didn't exist. His thinking was that if God existed, He wouldn't have allowed this to happen.

Now, you might say that this man's faith cannot have been very strong. Maybe he wouldn't have made a good pastor—who knows? But, unlike Abraham, he allowed his focus to move from God's call to his own personal problems. When we lose our heavenly perspective, we risk losing everything.

Adventures in Faith

Once we understand these three lessons—expect no guarantees, hold out for God's promises, and focus on the finish line—there is nothing to stop us from setting out on our own adventure in response to whatever God asks us to do. Unlike the religious lady who felt faith was too serious to talk about, we know that living by faith is exciting! With no guarantees except God's love and faithfulness, it may be time to set out on your own adventure of obedience and trust.

WORKBOOK

Chapter 12 Questions

Question: What promises of God can you focus on to help maintain your faithful walk with Jesus?

_____
_____
_____
_____
_____
_____
_____
_____
_____
_____
_____

Question: What hopes do you have for your future adventures in faith?

_____
_____
_____
_____
_____
_____
_____
_____
_____
_____
_____
_____

Action: A faith-filled life is an exciting adventure with no guarantees about where God will lead you or what you'll have to face. However, practicing your faith on a daily basis requires you to focus on the promises God is ready to fulfill after you reach the finish line.

Chapter 12 Notes

CONCLUSION

Going the Distance in Faith

This book has been about learning to exercise our faith—a process of self-discovery and God-discovery. We have compared it to a spiritual workout, a training regimen that has the potential to take us from a life of passive acceptance to one of energized commitment as we begin to exercise our faith muscles and move forward in our relationship with our Heavenly Father.

Of course, He forces none of us to embark on this journey. We can choose to slump back on our sofa and carry on as we were. God is a perfect gentleman and doesn't insist on this new level of commitment. But if we turn our backs on a life of faith, we won't be gaining anything by being fearful, too busy, or just plain lazy. In fact, we'll be missing out on so much!

What could God have in store for you? Could you be another Abraham, setting out for your own version of the Promised Land without knowing where that might be for you? Or a David, ready to take on God's enemies—as well as your own private battles against temptation and sin? Maybe, like Peter, Paul, and countless others, your journey into faith will lead you into places you would never have imagined as you witness His power at work in you and through you.

But as we know, "a journey of a thousand miles begins with a single step." Are you ready to get up off your spiritual sofa and take that first little step on your journey? Do you want to put your faith to work and get to know Him more?

Paul wrote to the Philippian church, "I want to know Christ—yes, to know the power of his resurrection and participation in his sufferings, becoming like him in his death, and so, somehow, attaining to the resurrection from the dead" (Philippians 3:10-11 NIV). Then Paul continues, "Forgetting what is behind and straining toward what is ahead, I press on toward the goal to win the prize for which God has called me heavenward in Christ Jesus" (Philippians 3:13-14 NIV).

On the day of Jesus's resurrection, two of the disciples were walking to Emmaus, a town outside Jerusalem, when they were joined by another walker. It was Jesus, although they didn't recognize Him for a while. As they continued together, Jesus walked beside them and taught them about Himself. Afterward, they said to each other, "Did not our heart burn within us while He talked with us on the road?" (Luke 24:32).

My friend, Jesus still accompanies His disciples as we get off the couch and begin our long-distance run down the road of faith. You will truly find you are not alone!

Notes

1. Richard J. Krejcir, "Discipleship: Understanding and Applying the Word," in *Into Thy Word* (2004), http://70030.netministry.com/apps/articles/defaul t.asp?articleid=32219&columnid=3844.
2. Ibid.
3. Thomas O. Chisholm, "Great Is Thy Faithfulness," 1923.
4. Isaac Watts, "Our God, Our Help in Ages Past," 1719.

About the Author

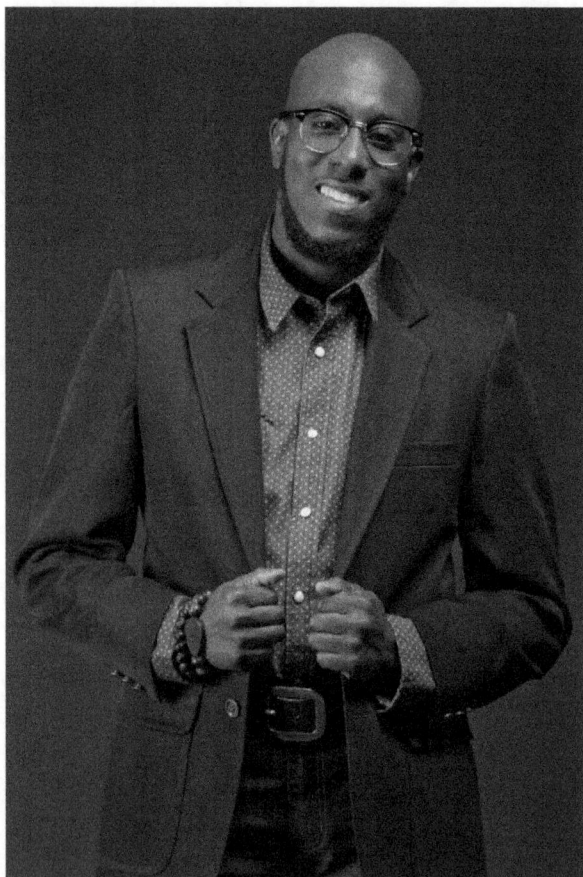

While other young adults ran from the call of God in their lives, Branddon A. Mays ran toward God's plan for his life. With a passion to empower all people despite generational, cultural, and denominational barriers, the Columbus, Georgia native was licensed in 2001 as an associate pastor by the late Rev. Raymond Mays, Sr. After serving within the youth ministry, overseeing and teaching Bible study at Corinth Missionary Baptist Church, Branddon was found faithful in his service and later received the call to pastor. In 2008, he was ordained by the late Rev. Raymond Mays, Sr., before launching his own ministry in 2009.

Launching ReVamp Church and BAM Ministries, Inc. in 2014, Dr. Mays has ministered to thousands. Committed to ministering to the total person—spirit, soul, and body—ReVamp Church exists to renew the mind, reenergize the faith of each person, and reconnect them to their God-given purpose. The ministry continues to thrive and experience rapid growth.

In addition to ReVamp Church and BAM Ministries, Inc., the ministry has developed various educational programs to equip believers. Under the direction of Dr. Mays, ReVamp Bible College was birthed and will launch in the fall of 2018.

Dr. Mays continues to pursue his God-given purpose by applying James 2:17, which states, "So too, faith, if it does not have works [to back it up], is by itself dead [inoperative and ineffective]" (AMP).

Since receiving his doctorate in divinity from St. Thomas Christian University in Jacksonville, Florida, Dr. Mays has served as the Chairperson of the Young Adult Division of the NAACP, Columbus, Georgia Chapter. During his year-long term, Dr. Mays assisted in the transformation of today's youth through their youth division.

He attributes his growth in the ministry to the teachings of his grandfather (the late Rev. Raymond Mays, Sr.) and the late Apostle Horace Leonard. Under the pastoral guidance of Bishop Norman

Hardman, pastor of Mount of Transfiguration in Opelika, Alabama, Dr. Mays has taken the teachings of these pioneers along with his anointing to deliver the Word of God through a nontraditional approach.

Dr. Mays will launch Vision In Action Coaching services in the summer of 2016. Vision In Action Coaching Services will bring life to every vision and help provide a strategy to each plan of action.

Dr. Mays has been blessed to minister across the country, touching the souls of the young and old. His deep commitment to reach the lost and embrace the forgotten with a relevant and intelligent message has given him a drive to see a rebirth of the Spirit and reconnection to God-given purpose within everyone he encounters.

Get in Touch with Branddon

Facebook: @brandmays

Twitter: @brandmays

Periscope: @brandmays

Instagram: brandmays

Website: www.brandmays.com

About Sermon to Book

SermonToBook.com began with a simple belief: that sermons should be touching lives, *not* collecting dust. That's why we turn sermons into high-quality books that are accessible to people all over the globe.

Turning your sermon series into a book exposes more people to God's Word, better equips you for counseling, accelerates future sermon prep, adds credibility to your ministry, and even helps make ends meet during tight times.

John 21:25 tells us that the world itself couldn't contain the books that would be written about the work of Jesus Christ. Our mission is to try anyway. Because, in Heaven, there will no longer be a need for sermons or books. Our time is now.

If God so leads you, we'd love to work with you on your sermon or sermon series.

Visit www.sermontobook.com to learn more.

www.ingramcontent.com/pod-product-compliance
Lightning Source LLC
LaVergne TN
LVHW051415080426
835508LV00022B/3098